RESOLUTE

MINDSET FOR MEN

RESOLUTE: Mindset For Men
Published by RESOLUTE
Author Vince Miller
Copyright © 2014 Resolute

Interior Design by Vince Miller
Interior Layout by Gretchen Miller
Cover Design and Layout by Eric Beavers
Printed by Ideal Printers

ISBN: 978-0-9982133-5-4

Printed in the United States of America

TABLE OF CONTENTS

SYSTEMS OF BELIEF   1

PERSPECTIVE   7

RENEWING YOUR MIND   13

KNOWING GOD   17

DESIRES & MOTIVATION   23

EVIL & SUFFERING   27

HOW TO USE THIS HANDBOOK

USE THIS HANDBOOK WITH OUR STREAMING VIDEOS.

As you navigate this guide, you will see that the lesson was designed for use with online streaming videos viewable only with a membership on our website at www.beresolute.org. The videos are what you will use to lead a group of men. Each lesson corresponds to a video. The best part is Vince Miller, our founder, has structured the streaming videos in such a way that they lead the time, so you don't have to. You do not have to prepare hours of content – he does it for you. If you are "hosting," all you need to do is push play and pause at the appropriate time and reference the content in the handbook.

ABOUT THE RESOLUTE METHOD.

At Resolute we provide you with a game plan. We are not just giving you content, but a method field-tested with hundreds of men. While the content is crucial, it is the method that is essential to spiritual change in a man's life. Each session has components we have tested that produce results in a man's life. In each lesson, you will notice clear goals and outcomes, purposeful discussion with other men, a rich study of God's Word, practical application, and a positive focus for 60-90 minutes. While we know, men enjoy our content; we hope this commitment to method deepens their relationship with Christ and one another.

THERE IS MORE CONTENT.

The series is not all the content you have access to with a membership. Also, we have stand-alone volumes to compliment this set. Check it out online. Or reach out to us at info@beresolute.org.

GETTING STARTED

The Resolute Directional Experience is designed to be a comprehensive discipleship plan for men. We have field-tested the Resolute method with hundreds of men over the last decade. It is intended to help men spiritually mature and has yielded proven results. Our program boasts of a complex logic model that is behavior-based and designed to nurture spiritual transformation for men through God's Word.

TO EFFECTIVELY USE THIS HANDBOOK

ONE | GATHER A TEAM.

Assembling a team is key. A team should include a pair of leaders who become the "On-Site Hosts" for the experience. We believe working in pairs is by far the most practical approach. Remember every Maverick needs a Goose.

TWO | RECRUIT MEN.

Don't stress. Whether you recruit half a dozen men or a hundred, the content will work efficiently. When recruiting, we have found the greatest success is finding men who are hungry to grow spiritually. While the content is good for any believer of any age, the best recruit is the one who wants to be there. These are what we call "hungry" men. To be clear these are men who hunger for the Word of God, and occasionally some food as well!

THREE | ENSURE EACH MAN HAS A HANDBOOK.

All our guides are purchased online at www.beresolute.org in the store. These are your guides for taking notes, guiding a dialogue with men in your group, and recording outcomes at the end of every lesson. Handbooks also include other materials for additional development. You will want one for each lesson series.

FOUR | LEADER ONLINE ENGAGEMENT.

If you are a leader and have purchased an online membership, you can view all the material. You will be able to listen to audio recaps, watch the videos, read the full transcripts, and even review past lessons.

FIVE | ACCESS MORE MATERIAL & RESOLUTE STAFF.

At Resolute we are not just selling curriculum. We are inviting you into an experience. Here are other tools for you to utilize.
• Men's Daily Devotionals.
• Men's Weekly Audio Podcasts.
You can also invite a representative from the Resolute to speak at your:
• Men's Group.
• Men's Retreat.
• Men's Breakfast.
It is our goal to partner with you and your men's ministry. We want to resource you with tools that compliment your development as a man of God and a leader.

SIX | CONNECT SOCIALLY.

We would love to have you join our social networks. Head to our home page www.beresolute.org and connect with us on Twitter, LinkedIn, and Facebook.

RESOLUTE

THE PRESENTER/AUTHOR

Vince Miller grew up on the west coast and was born in Vallejo, California where he spent all his childhood. At age 20, he made a profession of faith while in college and felt a sudden and strong call to work in full-time ministry. After college and graduate school, he invested two decades working with notable ministries like Young Life, InterVarsity Christian Fellowship, the local church, and in Senior Interim roles many times. He lives in St. Paul, Minnesota with Christina, his wife, and their three teenage children.

In March of 2014, he founded Resolute out of his passion for the discipleship and leadership development of men. This passion was born out of his own personal need for growth. Vince would say that he turned everywhere to find a man who would mentor, disciple, and develop him and over the course of his spiritual life and that he often received two answers from well-meaning Christian leaders – "Either they did not know what to do in a mentoring relationship, or they simply did not have the time to do it." Vince learned that he was not alone, and that many Christian men were seeking this type of mentorship relationship with another man. Out of this he felt compelled to build an organization that would focus on one thing, ensuring that men who want to be discipled have the opportunity, and that they can have real tools to disciple other men.

Vince is an authentic and transparent leader who loves to communicate to men and has a deep passion for God's Word. He has authored two books, The Generous Life and his newest book Convictions, which helps men understand how to close the gap between feeling convicted and living with conviction. And he is primary content creator of all Resolute content and training materials.

A PERSONAL NOTE FROM VINCE

I pray this experience will benefit your life and your spiritual journey as a man. I have three things that I hope you will do as you engage. First, that you will be receptive to the Word of God. I love, that we dig into the Bible every time we meet. The Bible is not an afterthought in Resolute – it is the means of discovering God and transformation. Second, lean into the brotherhood of this experience. Build friendships, share transparently, and have conversations that go beyond the superficial. Third, apply what you have learned. Take an action item with you every week, knowing that one small step weekly leads to success over a lifetime.

Keep moving forward,

SYSTEMS OF BELIEF

"As we first turned away from God in our thoughts, so it is in our thoughts that the first movements toward the renovation of the heart occur." – Dallas Willard.

"What comes into our minds when we think about God is the most important thing about us." – A.W. Tozer

SMALL GROUP DISCUSSION:

- Check in with each other.
- What is a corrupted belief you see in society today and why do you think people fall for this corrupted belief? (Consider the arenas of business, politics, education, religion, finance, etc.)
- How have you blown it lately? Consider a negative **behavior** or **emotion** and share it with your neighbor.
- Now share the **"corrupt" belief** that was driving this behavior or emotion.

INDUCTIVE STUDY

TEXT ONE

For though we walk in the flesh, we are not waging war according to the flesh. For the weapons of our warfare are not of the flesh but have divine power to destroy strongholds. We destroy arguments and every lofty opinion raised against the knowledge of God, and take every thought captive to obey Christ, being ready to punish every disobedience, when your obedience is complete.

2 CORINTHIANS 10:3-6

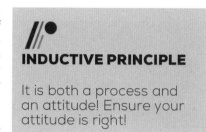

INDUCTIVE PRINCIPLE

It is both a process and an attitude! Ensure your attitude is right!

TEXT TWO

For who knows a person's thoughts except the spirit of that person, which is in him? So also no one comprehends the thoughts of God except the Spirit of God. Now we have received not the spirit of the world, but the Spirit who is from God, that we might understand the things freely given us by God. And we impart this in words not taught by human wisdom but taught by the Spirit, interpreting spiritual truths to those who are spiritual. The natural person does not accept the things of the Spirit of God, for they are folly to him, and he is not able to understand them because they are spiritually discerned. The spiritual person judges all things, but is himself to be judged by no one. "For who has understood the mind of the LORD so as to instruct him?" But we have the mind of Christ.

1 CORINTHIANS 2:11-16

TEXT THREE

What then? Are we Jews any better off? No, not at all. For we have already charged that all, both Jews and Greeks, are under sin, as it is written: "None is righteous, no, not one; no one understands; no one seeks for God. All have turned aside; together they have become worthless; no one does good, not even one. "Their throat is an open grave; they use their tongues to deceive." "The venom of asps is under their lips." "Their mouth is full of curses and bitterness." "Their feet are swift to shed blood; in their paths are ruin and misery, and the way of peace they have not known." "There is no fear of God before their eyes." Now we know that whatever the law says it speaks to those who are under the law, so that every mouth may be stopped, and the whole world may be held accountable to God. For by works of the law no human being will be justified in his sight, since through the law comes knowledge of sin.

ROMANS 3:9-19

TEXT FOUR

"For those who live according to the flesh set their minds on the things of the flesh, but those who live according to the Spirit set their minds on the things of the Spirit. For to set the mind on the flesh is death, but to set the mind on the Spirit is life and peace. For the mind that is set on the flesh is hostile to God, for it does not submit to God's law; indeed, it cannot. Those who are in the flesh cannot please God."

ROMANS 8:5-8

FOUR PRINCIPLES ABOUT BELIEF SYSTEMS

PRINCIPLE ONE: We _____ belief systems.

"For my thoughts are not your thoughts, neither are your ways my ways, declares the LORD."
– Isaiah 55:8

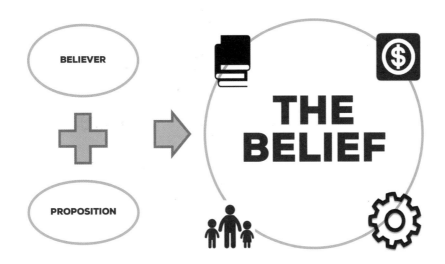

PRINCIPLE TWO: We are _____ by our belief systems.

"For as he thinks within himself, so he is." – Proverbs 23:7

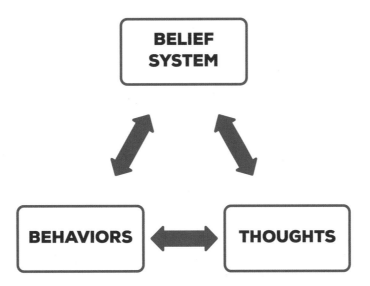

RESOLUTE

PRINCIPLE THREE: We have
_____ belief sys-
tems.

"The LORD saw that the wickedness of
man was great in the earth, and that
every intention of the thoughts of his
heart was only evil continually." – Genesis 6:5

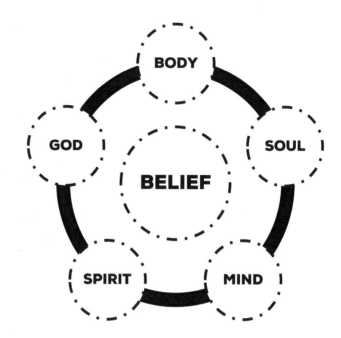

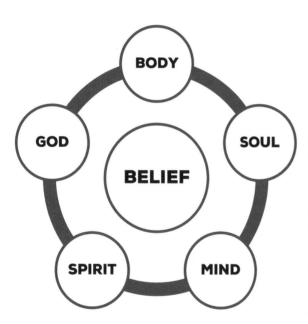

PRINCIPLE FOUR: God must _____ the
belief system.

"Jesus said to him, "I am the way, and the truth, and
the life. No one comes to the Father except through
me." – John 14:6

MY ACTION ITEMS:

What issue needs addressing in my beliefs? What
steps do I take to alter this?

READ: Galatians

SKILL DEVELOPMENT // BIBLE READING

Do an inductive study of Galatians 1:1-10. Read the rest of Galatians over the course of the week (1-2 chapters per day).

PERSPECTIVE

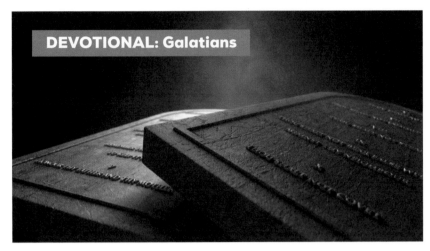

DEVOTIONAL: Galatians

"We are not human beings having a spiritual experience. We are spiritual beings having a human experience." – Pierre Teilhard de Chardin

"Often it isn't the mountains ahead that wear you out, it's the little pebble in your shoe."
— Muhammad Ali

"For what you see and hear depends a good deal on where you are standing: it also depends on what sort of person you are." — C. S. Lewis

SMALL GROUP DISCUSSION:

- Check in with each other.
- Where is the most unusual or highest elevation you have ever been? What was your vantage point like from that angle looking down on your surroundings?
- What is the most spectacular experience you have had in life? What changed in your vantage point after this experience?
- What do you think about yourself spiritually on most days? (Be open and honest.)

RESOLUTE

IN LIGHT OF LAST WEEK

God's Vantage Point of Humanity:

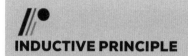
INDUCTIVE PRINCIPLE

As you approach the text say to yourself, "God I will do whatever you would have me do whether I agree or disagree!"

9 What then? Are we Jews any better off? No, not at all. For we have already charged that all, both Jews and Greeks, are under sin, 10 as it is written: "None is righteous, no, not one; 11 no one understands; no one seeks for God. 12 All have turned aside; together they have become worthless; no one does good, not even one. 13 "Their throat is an open grave; they use their tongues to deceive." "The venom of asps is under their lips." 14 "Their mouth is full of curses and bitterness." 15 "Their feet are swift to shed blood; 16 in their paths are ruin and misery, 17 and the way of peace they have not known." 18 "There is no fear of God before their eyes."

ROMANS 3:9-18

OUR INDUCTIVE STUDY

God Vantage Point of Me Through Christ:

1 Paul, an apostle of Christ Jesus by the will of God, to the saints who are in Ephesus, and are faithful in Christ Jesus: 2 Grace to you and peace from God our Father and the LORD Jesus Christ. 3 Blessed be the God and Father of our LORD Jesus Christ, who has blessed us in Christ with every spiritual blessing in the heavenly places, 4 even as he chose us in him before the foundation of the world, that we should be holy and blameless before him. In love 5 he predestined us for adoption as sons through Jesus Christ, according to the purpose of his will, 6 to the praise of his glorious grace, with which he has blessed us in the Beloved. 7 In him we have redemption through his blood, the forgiveness of our trespasses, according to the riches of his grace, 8 which he lavished upon us, in all wisdom and insight 9 making known to us the mystery of his will, according to his purpose, which he set forth in Christ 10 as a plan for the fullness of time, to unite all things in him, things in heaven and things on earth. 11 In him we have obtained an inheritance, having been predestined according to the purpose of him who works all things according to the counsel of his will, 12 so that we who were the first to hope in Christ might be to the praise of his glory. 13 In him you also, when you heard the word of truth, the gospel of your salvation, and believed in him, were sealed with the promised Holy Spirit, 14 who is the guarantee of our inheritance until we acquire possession of it, to the praise of his glory.

EPHESIANS 1:1-14

THE FIVE MEN WE ARE | Perspectives:

- **#1:** The man we think we are.
- **#2:** The man others think we are.
- **#3:** The man we think others think we are.
- **#4:** The man we actually are. ------------------------ Romans 3
- **#5:** The man God views us to be. -------------------- Ephesians 1

"For as he thinks within himself, so is he." Proverbs 23:7

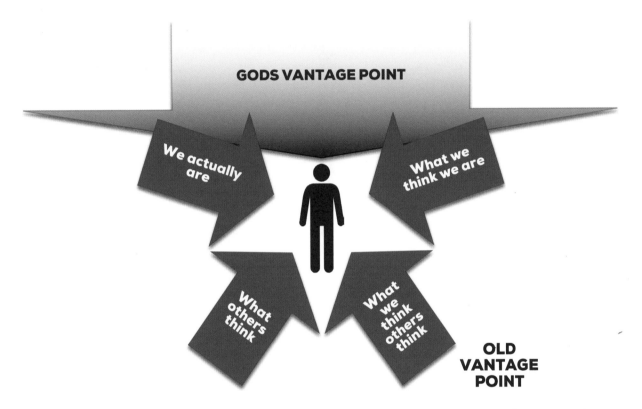

THE KEY TO THINKING LIKE A DISCIPLE IS DEVELOPING A NEW SOURCE FOR YOUR BELIEF SYSTEM

THE MEN GOD SAYS WE ARE:

• **I am a child of God.** "But to all who have received him--those who believe in his name--he has given the right to become God's children."(John 1:12).

• **I am conduit of Christ's life.** "I am the true vine and my Father is the gardener. I am the vine; you are the branches. The one who remains in me--and I in him--bears much fruit, because apart from me you can accomplish nothing." (John 15:1, 5).

• **I am a friend of Jesus.** "I no longer call you slaves, because the slave does not understand what his master is doing. But I have called you friends, because I have revealed to you everything I heard from my Father." (John 15:15).

• **I am justified and redeemed.** "But they are justified freely by his grace through the redemption that is in Christ Jesus." (Romans 3:24).

• **I am no longer a slave to sin.** "We know that our old man was crucified with him so that the body of sin would no longer dominate us, so that we would no longer be enslaved to sin." (Romans 6:6).

• **I am not condemned.** "There is therefore now no condemnation for those who are in Christ Jesus." (Romans 8:1).

• **I have been set free from death.** "For the law of the life-giving Spirit in Christ Jesus has set you free from the law of sin and death." (Romans 8:2).

• **I am a fellow heir.** "And if children, then heirs (namely, heirs of God and also fellow heirs with Christ)--if indeed we suffer with him so we may also be glorified with him." (Romans 8:17).

• **I have been accepted.** "Receive one another, then, just as Christ also received you, to God's glory." (Romans 15:7).

• **I am called to be a saint.** "To the church of God that is in Corinth, to those who are sanctified in Christ Jesus, and called to be saints, with all those in every place who call on the name of our LORD Jesus Christ, their LORD and ours." (1 Corinthians 1:2).

• **I have wisdom, righteousness, sanctification, and redemption.** "He is the reason you have a relationship with Christ Jesus, who became for us wisdom from God, and righteousness and sanctification and redemption." (1 Corinthians 1:30).

• **I am a temple of the Holy Spirit.** "Do you not know that you are God's temple and that God's Spirit lives in you?" (1 Corinthians 6:19)

• **I am a new creation.** "So then, if anyone is in Christ, he is a new creation; what is old has passed away--look, what is new has come!" (2 Corinthians 5:17).

• **I have become the righteousness of God.** "God made the one who did not know sin to be sin for us, so that in him we would become the righteousness of God." (2 Corinthians 5:21).

MY ACTION ITEMS:

Issues to Address. Steps to Take.

What issue above needs to be addressed in my perspective? What steps do I need to take to ensure it aligns with God's Truth and Word?

READ: Ephesians

SKILL DEVELOPMENT // BIBLE READING

Do an inductive study of Ephesians 1:1-14. Read chapters 2-6 over the remainder of the week.

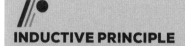
RENEWING YOUR MIND

DEVOTIONAL: Ephesians

SMALL GROUP DISCUSSION:

- Check in with each other.
- As you were growing up was there ever a major transformation you went through physically, mentally, or emotionally? What was this like for you?
- What has been the most transformational lesson or moment from our time together in the last 14 weeks? Why?
- What do you think would be among the most damaging thoughts that people have about God that keep them from believing? (List them.)
- What is your biggest pet peeve? Why is it this?

INDUCTIVE PRINCIPLE

Everyone brings a presupposition to the text. It is uncovering these and allowing God to correct that leads to deepening obedience.

1 I appeal to you therefore, brothers, by the mercies of God, to present your bodies as a living sacrifice, holy and acceptable to God, which is your spiritual worship. 2 Do not be conformed to this world, but be transformed by the renewal of your mind, that by testing you may discern what is the will of God, what is good and acceptable and perfect. 3 For by the grace given to me I say to everyone among you not to think of himself more highly than he ought to think, but to think with sober judgment, each according to the measure of faith that God has assigned.

ROMANS 12:1-3

17 Now this I say and testify in the LORD, that you must no longer walk as the Gentiles do, in the futility of their minds. 18 They are darkened in their understanding, alienated from the life of God because of the ignorance that is in them, due to their hardness of heart. 19 They have become callous and have given themselves up to sensuality, greedy to practice every kind of impurity. 20 But that is not the way you learned Christ! 21 assuming that you have heard about him and were taught in him, as the truth is in Jesus, 22 to put off your old self, which belongs to your former manner of life and is corrupt through deceitful desires, 23 and to be renewed in the spirit of your minds, 24 and to put on the new self, created after the likeness of God in true righteousness and holiness.

EPHESIANS 4:17-24

THE IMPORTANCE OF RENEWING THE MIND:

"What comes into our minds when we think about God is the most important thing about us.... For this reason the gravest question before the Church is always God Himself, and the most portentous fact about any man is not what he at a given time may say or do, but what he in his deep heart conceives God to be like. We tend by a secret law of the soul to move toward our mental image of God.

Were we able to extract from any man a complete answer to the question, "What comes into your mind when you think about God?" we might predict with certainty the spiritual future of that man... Without doubt, the mightiest thought the mind can entertain is the thought of God, and the weightiest word in any language is its word for God...

That our idea of God corresponds as nearly as possible to the true being of God is of immense importance to us. Compared with our actual thoughts about Him, our creedal statements are of little consequence. Our real idea of God may lie buried under the rubbish of conventional religious notions and may require an intelligent and vigorous search before it is finally unearthed and exposed for what it is. Only after an ordeal of painful self-probing are we likely to discover what we actually believe about God."

A.W. TOZER, THE KNOWLEDGE OF THE HOLY.

AMERICA'S FOUR GODS,

By Paul Froese and Christopher Bader. (Baylor University Professors, 2010)

28% - "**Authoritative God**," A God who is judgmental and yet very engaged in the world at the same time.

22% - "**Benevolent God**," A God who is thoroughly involved in their lives yet is loving and not stern. Just a friend that is there when you need him.

21% - "**Critical God**," A God who is removed from daily events and will render a strong judgment in the afterlife.

24% - "**Distant God**," A God who set the world in motion and then disengaged. These people tend to call themselves spiritual but not religious.

MY ACTION ITEMS:

Issues to Address. Steps to Take.

What is an action you would like to change and what is the bad thinking you have wrongly believed that led to it? What steps do you need to take to address this?

SKILL DEVELOPMENT // BIBLE READING

READ: Philippians

Do inductive study of Philippians 1:1-11. Read chapters 2-4 over the remaining days.

KNOWING GOD

DEVOTIONAL: Philippians

INDUCTIVE PRINCIPLE

God's Word is revealed outside of humanity (objective) and yet realized inside of us (subjective).

John 7:17 – "My teaching is not mine, but his who sent me. "

5 Thomas said to him, "LORD, we do not **know** where you are going. How can we **know** the way?" 6 Jesus said to him, "I am the way, and the truth, and the life. No one comes to the Father except through me. 7 If you had **known** me, you would have **known** my Father also. From now on you do **know** him and have seen him."

8 Philip said to him, "LORD, show us the Father, and it is enough for us." 9 Jesus said to him, "Have I been with you so long, and you still do not **know** me, Philip? Whoever has seen me has seen the Father. How can you say, 'Show us the Father'? 10 Do you not believe that I am in the Father and the Father is in me? The words that I say to you I do not speak on my own authority, but the Father who dwells in me does his works. 11 Believe me that I am in the Father and the Father is in me, or else believe on account of the works themselves.

JOHN 14:5-11

DEFINING WORDS:

5 "For God **knows** that when you eat of it your eyes will be opened, and you will be like God, **knowing** good and evil." – Genesis 3:5

7 "Then the eyes of both were opened, and they **knew** that they were naked. And they sewed fig leaves together and made themselves loincloths." – Genesis 3:7

22 "Then the LORD God said, "Behold, the man has become like one of us in **knowing** good and evil." – Genesis 3:22

1 "Now Adam **knew** Eve his wife, and she conceived and bore Cain, saying, "I have gotten a man with the help of the LORD." – Genesis 4:1

19 "For I have **chosen** him, that he may command his children and his household after him to keep the way of the LORD by doing righteousness and justice, so that the LORD may bring to Abraham what he has promised him." – Genesis 18:19

SMALL GROUP DISCUSSION:

- Check in with each other.
- Who is a big leader (living or dead) you would love to meet?
- If you were invited to eat at a large event featuring this leader what would be your initial response to an invite of this nature?
- How would your view of this leader change if he were to invite you to privately have dinner with him and he were to open-up with you about the personal challenges he was facing?

KNOWING IN ANCIENT HEBREW (OT)

Yada is the Hebrew word for knowing.

- "For God knows (yada)"
- "Knowing (yada) good and evil."
- "They knew (yada) that they were naked."
- "Become like one of us in knowing (yada) good and evil.
- "Now Adam knew (yada) Eve"
- "For I have chosen (yada) him,"

יָדַע "Yada."

This Hebrew verb has a range of meaning from knowing something intellectually (information) to being sexually intimate (acquaintance with relationally, emotionally, physically, spiritually). In a legal context, it refers to the faithful relationship of two things, parties, or people. So it can mean to perceive, to know intimately, to understand, or to experience.

KNOWING IN ANCIENT GREEK (NT)

₅ "Thomas said to him, 'LORD, we do not **know** (oida) where you are going. How can we **know** (oida) the way?'"

₇ "If you had **known** (ginōskō) me, you would have **known** (ginōskō) my Father also. From now on you do **know** (ginōskō) him and have seen him." ₈ Philip said to him, "LORD, show us the Father, and it is enough for us." ₉ Jesus said to him, "Have I been with you so long, and you still do not **know** (ginōskō) me, Philip?"

Thomas Says & Philip Thinks:

οἶδα **(oida)** - To know; to know how.

Jesus Thinks & Says:

γινώσκω **(ginōskō)** - A full knowing.

A.W. TOZER

"Left to ourselves we tend immediately to reduce God to manageable terms. We want to get Him where we can use Him, or at least know where He is when we need Him. We want a God we can in some measure control. We need the feeling of security that comes from knowing what God is like, and what He is like of course a composite of all religious pictures we have seen, all the best people we have known or heard about, and all the sublime ideas we have entertained."

RESOLUTE

THE KEY IDEA:

Three general types of knowing:

- **Propositional** knowledge: "know that"
- **Process** knowledge: "know how"
- **Personal** knowledge: "know by acquaintance"

A small amount of **personal** knowledge of God is worth more than a ton of **propositional** & **process** knowledge about God. Therefore, we can reverse this statement and say that we can know a lot of **propositions** & **processes** about God but fail to know God **personally**. This is the case for many Christians who have never become disciples. Therefore, we can know God **personally** without a deep knowledge about God or we could even say we could be very "Godly" without a deep knowledge about "that" or "how." Mark 10:14-16 below is an example of this.

₁₄ "But when Jesus saw it, he was indignant and said to them, "Let the children come to me; do not hinder them, for to such belongs the kingdom of God. ₁₅ Truly, I say to you, whoever does not receive the kingdom of God like a child shall not enter it." ₁₆ And he took them in his arms and blessed them, laying his hands on them." – Mark 10:14-16

QUESTION:

- Do we understand to believe or do we believe to understand?
- Do we see to believe or believe to see?

FIVE FACTORS THAT WE KNOW GOD (PERSONALLY):

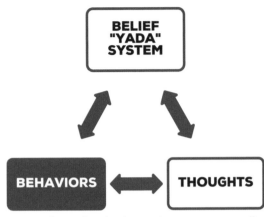

If evidence of our discipleship is not "knowing that" or "knowing how" then what is our evidence? Would our evidence not be **obedience** or **behaviors** that are outputs from the disciple who knows personally? Here are 5 evidences of the disciple who knows God.

1.   Those who "yada" God show **boldness for** God. ₃₂ *"And David said to Saul, "Let no man's heart fail because of him. Your servant will go and fight with this Philistine."* ₃₃ *And Saul said to David, "You are not able to go against this Philistine to fight with him, for you are but a youth, and he has been a man of war from his youth."* ₃₄ *But David said to Saul, "Your servant used to keep sheep for his father. And when there came a lion, or a bear, and took a lamb from the flock,* ₃₅ *I went after him and struck him and delivered it out of his mouth. And if he arose against me, I caught him by his beard and struck him and killed him.* ₃₆ *Your servant has struck down both lions and bears, and this uncircumcised Philistine shall be like one of them, for he has defied the armies of the living God.* ₃₇ *And David said, "The LORD who delivered me from the paw of the lion and from the paw of the bear will deliver me from the hand of this Philistine."* – 1 Samuel 17:32-37

2.   Those who "yada" God have a **message about** God. ₃₈ *"For I am sure that neither death nor life, nor angels nor rulers, nor things present nor things to come, nor powers,* ₃₉ *nor height nor depth, nor anything else in all creation, will be able to separate us from the love of God in Christ Jesus our LORD."* – Romans 8:38-39

3.   Those who "yada" God have a **supernatural effort for** God. ₃₂ *"He shall seduce with flattery those who violate the covenant, but the people who **know** their God shall stand firm and take action."* – Daniel 11:32

4.   Those who "yada" God have an **intimacy with** God. ₁₀ *"That I may **know** him and the power of his resurrection, and may share his sufferings, becoming like him in his death,"* – Philippians 3:10

5.   Those who "yada" God have a **reverence to** God. ₁₀ *"Be still, and **know** that I am God. I will be exalted among the nations, I will be exalted in the earth!"* – Psalm 46:10

MY ACTION ITEMS:

Issues to Address. Steps to Take.

Which of the five factors above do you need to address? What steps do you need to take to improve this?

READ: Colossians

SKILL DEVELOPMENT // BIBLE READING

Do inductive study of Colossians 1:1-14. Read the remainder of Colossians over the remaining days.

DESIRES & MOTIVATION

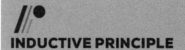

INDUCTIVE PRINCIPLE

Study done in community has farther-reaching implications especially when interpreting – both actively and passively.

SMALL GROUP DISCUSSION:

- Check in with each other.
- What is your favorite meal? Describe this meal in detail including protein, vegetable, bread, etc.
- What is the most important task you must get done today? Why is this of highest importance? What is driving you to get this done?
- What is one area of your life where you lack self-control? Why is this an issue? What is the trigger that sets this off?

16 But I say, walk by the Spirit, and you will not gratify the desires of the flesh. 17 For the desires of the flesh are against the Spirit, and the desires of the Spirit are against the flesh, for these are opposed to each other, to keep you from doing the things you want to do. 18 But if you are led by the Spirit, you are not under the law. 19 Now the works of the flesh are evident: sexual immorality, impurity, sensuality, 20 idolatry, sorcery, enmity, strife, jealousy, fits of anger, rivalries, dissensions, divisions, 21 envy, drunkenness, orgies, and things like these. I warn you, as I warned you before, that those who do such things will not inherit the kingdom of God. 22 But the fruit of the Spirit is love, joy, peace, patience, kindness, goodness, faithfulness, 23 gentleness, self-control; against such things there is no law. 24 And those who belong to Christ Jesus have crucified the flesh with its passions and desires. 25 If we live by the Spirit, let us also keep in step with the Spirit. 26 Let us not become conceited, provoking one another, envying one another.

GALATIANS 5:16-26

DEVOTIONAL: Colossians

RESOLUTE

GREEK WORD FOR DESIRE:

ἐπιθυμία "**epithymía**" **(n)** – Passion built on strong feelings (urges). These can be positive or negative, depending on whether the desire is inspired by faith.

ἐπιθυμέω "**epithumeó**" **(v)** - I long for, covet, lust after, set the heart upon.

- **"epi"** – focused on
- **"thymos"** – passionate desire

There are several interchangeable English words that convey the Greek concept of desire. Words like "desire, earnest, lust, passion, and covet." These words can be stated **positively** or **negatively**. They also can be **internally** or **externally** motivated. We should also note that desire involves different parts of the disciple including the heart, mind, soul, spirit and will. There is a clear war between body (fleshly) desires and the Spirit (Holy Spirit) within us. And last, that God wants our full focus when it comes to our desire.

TYPES OF MOTIVATION:

INTRINSIC MOTIVATION

IN-
- I don't [XXXX] nor do I care.

IN +
- I [XXXX] because I love God.

NEGATIVE MOTIVE

POSITIVE MOTIVE

EX -
- I [XXXX] because if I don't God will get mad.

EX+
- I [XXXX] because people will appluad me.

EXTRINSIC MOTIVATION

RESOLUTE

THE POWER OF THE RUDDER OF DESIRE:

Desire is a rudder that has the power to direct our life. This "focused passion" will direct our flesh toward sin or direct our flesh toward God. Desires are powerful. Appropriately directed desires can lead to very positive results and inappropriately directed desires can lead to destructive results. But how do we reorient them?

THE PROCESS OF REDIRECTING OUR DESIRES:

Write down one misplaced desire you have here:

FIRST | DECIDE. Make the conscious decision you are no longer going to tolerate this sin and that you are tired of your sins and desires directing your life.

SECOND | DESCRIBE & IDENTIFY. Next you want to describe what happens when this sin or misplace desire occurs. **Describe** the environment and emotions you feel. Describe it in as much detail as possible. You are attempting to **identify** two things. First the **trigger** and the **reward**. The trigger is the thing that keeps setting the sin off, the reward is why you keep repeating the sin. You must get a good handle on the reward because this is what keeps you coming back for more! Every sin has a powerful but short-lived reward.

JAMES 1:12-15

12 "Blessed is the man who remains steadfast under trial, for when he has stood the test he will receive the crown of life, which God has promised to those who love him. 13 Let no one say when he is tempted, "I am being tempted by God," for God cannot be tempted with evil, and he himself tempts no one. 14 But each person is tempted when he is lured and enticed by his own desire. 15 Then desire when it has conceived gives birth to sin, and sin when it is fully grown brings forth death."

THIRD | MAKE ADVANCE DECISIONS. Next you are going to decide in advance the next time this trigger or misplaced desire arises. It only needs to be a simple decision but make it now, so you do not have to guess about what you are going to do the next time the trigger arises.

FOURTH | A NEW REWARD. You cannot only discipline negative desires, since desires are also positive. You must simultaneously **redirect** them because there is no neutrality between desires of flesh and the Spirit. God wants you to have desires but he wants the "focused on passion" on Him. The best choice here is counteracting the negative desire with a Godly desire and a spiritual reward.

MY ACTION ITEMS:

- What is the misplaced desire you would like to address?
- What conscious decisions do you need to make about your misplaced desire?
- What is the trigger and the reward of the sin? Describe in detail.
- What decision do you need to make in advance?
- What Godly reward counteracts your fleshly reward?

READ: 1 Thessalonians

SKILL DEVELOPMENT // BIBLE READING

Read 1 Thessalonians over the course of the week. Choose 2 sections to study inductively.

EVIL & SUFFERING

DEVOTIONAL: 1 Thessalonians

₁ And Jesus, full of the Holy Spirit, returned from the Jordan and was led by the Spirit in the wilderness ₂ for forty days, being tempted by the devil. And he ate nothing during those days. And when they were ended, he was hungry. ₃ The devil said to him, "If you are the Son of God, command this stone to become bread." ₄ And Jesus answered him, "It is written, 'Man shall not live by bread alone.'"

₅ And the devil took him up and showed him all the kingdoms of the world in a moment of time, ₆ and said to him, "To you I will give all this authority and their glory, for it has been delivered to me, and I give it to whom I will. ₇ If you, then, will worship me, it will all be yours." ₈ And Jesus answered him, "It is written, '"You shall worship the LORD your God, and him only shall you serve.'"

₉ And he took him to Jerusalem and set him on the pinnacle of the temple and said to him, "If you are the Son of God, throw yourself down from here, ₁₀ for it is written, "'He will command his angels concerning you, to guard you,' ₁₁ and "'On their hands they will bear you up, lest you strike your foot against a stone.'" ₁₂ And Jesus answered him, "It is said, 'You shall not put the LORD your God to the test.'"

₁₃ And when the devil had ended every temptation, he departed from him until an opportune time.

LUKE 4:1-13

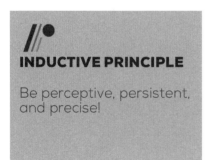

INDUCTIVE PRINCIPLE

Be perceptive, persistent, and precise!

SMALL GROUP DISCUSSION:

- Check in with each other.
- What is the longest time you have lived away from the comforts of civilization?
- What are the greatest temptations for men today?
- What is the "test" that you are currently facing?

WHY EVIL IS A "PROBLEM?"

The key issue in discussing the problem of evil is how to reconcile the existence of evil with that of any deity specifically in this case the Triune God. An argument against God from a position of the problem of evil or suffering attempts to show that the co-existence of evil and such a deity is unlikely or impossible if placed in absolute terms.

DEFINITION OF EVIL & SUFFERING:

- **Evil** is any action, thought, or attitude that is contrary to the character or will of God.
- **Suffering** is to feel or bear what is painful or distressing to the body or mind.

COMMON MISUNDERSTANDINGS OF EVIL:

1. **Evil is a thing or a being.** Evil is <u>not</u> either, a <u>thing</u> or a <u>being</u>. Things are not evil. Human beings are not evil. If they were the problem of evil would be impossible to solve. The evil is in "the will" or "the intent" of the person holding the gun. Therefore, evil is real (objective) but evil is not a real thing (entity).

2. **Confusing Physical Evil and Moral Evil.** These are two different types of evil that often are confused or misunderstood.

MORAL EVIL	PHYSICAL EVIL
• Sin.	• Suffering.
• The evil we actively do.	• The evil we passively suffer.
• The evil we freely will.	• The evil that is against our will.
• The evil we are responsible for.	• The evil we are not responsible for.

AUGUSTINE (A.D. 354-430)

Augustine stated that **physical evil** (evil present such as natural disasters) is caused by fallen angels, whereas **moral evil** (evil caused by the will of human beings) is a result of man having become estranged from God and choosing to deviate from his chosen path. Augustine argued that God could not have created evil in the world, as it was created good.

C.S. LEWIS (A.D. 1898-1963)

"My argument against God was that the universe seemed so cruel and unjust. But how had I got this idea of just and unjust? A man does not call a line crooked unless he has some idea of a straight line. What was I comparing this universe with when I called it unjust? Of course, I could have given up my idea of justice by saying it was nothing but a private idea of my own. But if I did that, then my argument against God collapsed too—for the argument depended on saying the world was unjust, not simply that it did not happen to please my fancies."

READ: 2 Thessalonians Take the Spiritual Gifts Assessment at <u>beresolute.org/sga</u>

SKILL DEVELOPMENT // BIBLE READING

Read 2 Thessalonians over the course of the week. Choose 2 sections to study inductively.